TOPPERS
Ocean Animals

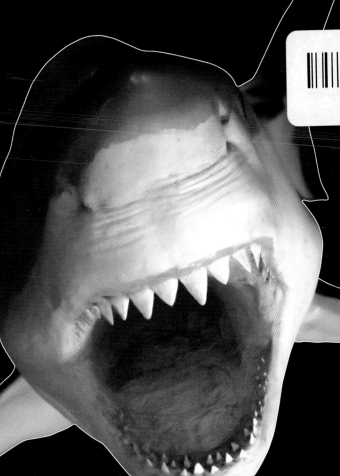

Created by Q2AMedia

www.q2amedia.com

Text, design & illustrations Copyright © Leopard Learning 2009

Editor Jessica Cohn
Publishing Director Chester Fisher
Client Service Manager Santosh Vasudevan
Project Manager Shekhar Kapur
Art Director Sumit Charles
Designer Divya Jain and Joita Das
Illustrator Ajay Sharma and Vinay Kumar
Art Editor Mariea Janet
Picture Researcher Shreya Sharma

10 9 8 7 6 5 4 3 2 1

ISBN: 81-905723-7-7

Printed in China

Picture Credits

t= top, bg= background, bl= bottom left, br= bottom right, tl= top left, tr= top right

Cover Images: Front: Rena Schild: Shutterstock. tr Mikhail Blajenov:Dreamstime

Half Title: Ian Scott:BigStockPhoto

4-5bg Dreamstime. 4bl Shutterstock. 5br1 Shutterstock. 5br2 John A. Anderson: Shutterstock. 6-7 Reinhard Dirscherl: Photolibrary. 7t

Mikhail Blajenov: Dreamstime. 8-9 Shutterstock. 8 David Shale: naturepl.com. 9br Oxford Scientific: Photolibrary. 10-11 Shutterstock. 10 Ian Scott: BigStockPhoto. 11t Ian Scott: Shutterstock. 11b Tania A: Shutterstock. 12 Iurii Sobolevsky: Dreamstime. 13 Olga Khoroshunova: Fotolia. 14-15 Rena Schild: Shutterstock. 15b David B Fleetham: Photolibrary. 16-17 Christopher Waters: Shutterstock. 16 Shutterstock. 17 John Anderson: Dreamstime. 18 Eric Isselée: Dreamstime. 19 Dreamstime. 20 Dreamstime. 21 iStockphoto. 22 Michael Patrick O'neill: NHPA. 23

Shutterstock. 24 Shutterstock. 25 Kim Reinick: 123RF. 26 Trevor Allen: Fotolia. 27 Yang Jay: Dreamstime. 28 Expedition to the Deep Slope 2006 Exploration: NOAA. 29 Tobias Bernhard: Photolibrary. 30-31bg Dreamstime. 31b Rena Schild: Shutterstock

CD Credits: Shutterstock and iStockphoto

Table of Contents

World of Water

The ocean is very, very big. It is filled with wonderful animals. Some swim. Some crawl along the bottom. Some live near the shore. We will learn about some ocean animals in this book.

FISH

MOLLUSKS

MAMMALS

CRUSTACEANS

These four animal groups live in the ocean.

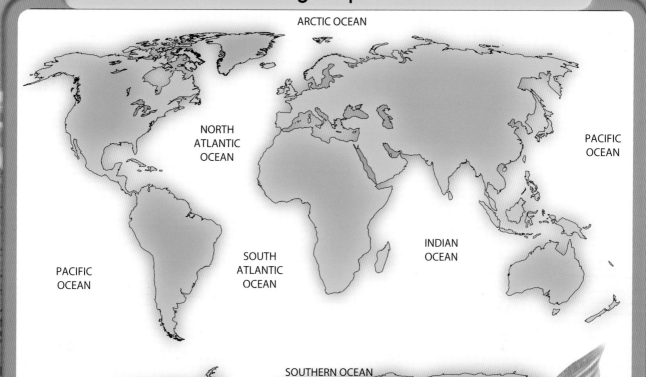

ARCTIC OCEAN

NORTH ATLANTIC OCEAN

PACIFIC OCEAN

PACIFIC OCEAN

SOUTH ATLANTIC OCEAN

INDIAN OCEAN

SOUTHERN OCEAN

FACTS

- **Most of the Earth (70 percent) is covered by ocean.**
- **Different parts of the ocean have different names.**

5

Angelfish

FACTS

- An angelfish lays egg in plants on the bottom of the ocean.
- An angelfish is not afraid of swimming right up to people.
- Many people keep angelfish as pets.

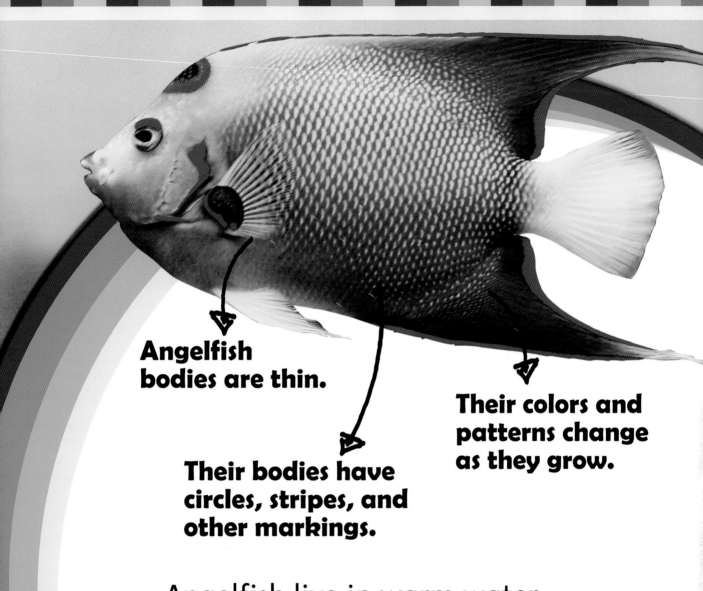

Angelfish bodies are thin.

Their bodies have circles, stripes, and other markings.

Their colors and patterns change as they grow.

Angelfish live in warm water. They look like colorful rainbows when they swim. Fish like angelfish swim in large groups called **schools**. A whole school can change direction at once.

FISH

Viperfish

This part acts like a flashlight.

FACTS

- Viperfish live deep in the ocean. There is very little light there.
- These fish can make their own light!
- They use their light to get the attention of fish they want to eat.

Viperfish are scary-looking. They have long, sharp teeth. Their teeth are too big for their mouths! Some viperfish are all black. Others are clear. You can see right through them!

A wide mouth helps it eat big fish.

Big eyes help it see in the dark.

Shark

A shark grows as many as 20,000 teeth.

Its jaws are the most powerful of any animal.

FISH

Sharks are large fish with sharp teeth. Sharks eat anything that swims, even other sharks! Some sharks zoom through the ocean as they hunt. Others hide on the bottom and strike when ready.

FACTS

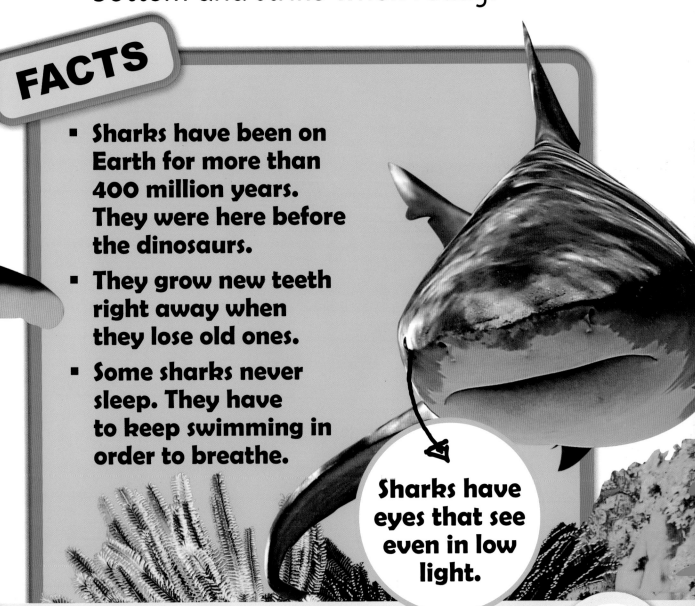

- **Sharks have been on Earth for more than 400 million years. They were here before the dinosaurs.**
- **They grow new teeth right away when they lose old ones.**
- **Some sharks never sleep. They have to keep swimming in order to breathe.**

Sharks have eyes that see even in low light.

MOLLUSKS

Cuttlefish

Cuttlefish are not fish! They are animals called **mollusks.**

Cuttlefish change color to send messages to other cuttlefish. They can also make themselves the color of sand. The sandy color helps them hide from sharks and seals.

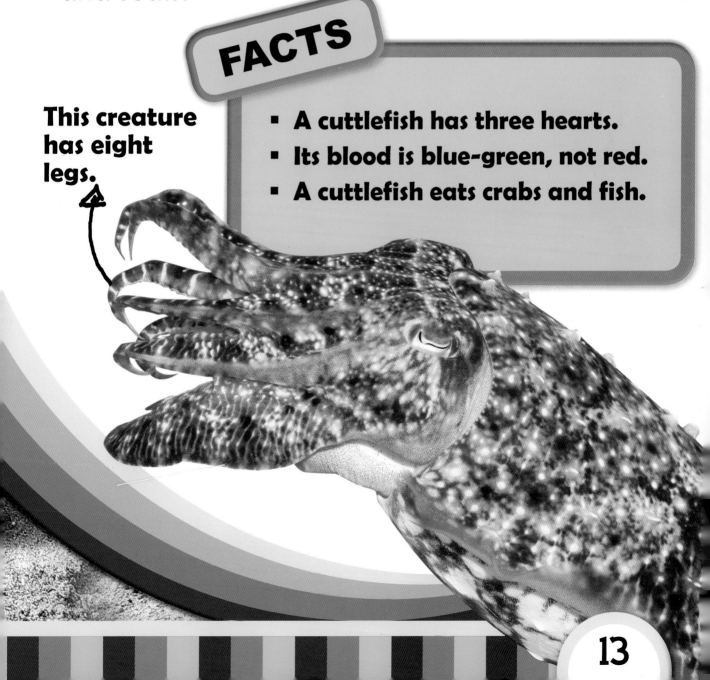

FACTS

This creature has eight legs.

- **A cuttlefish has three hearts.**
- **Its blood is blue-green, not red.**
- **A cuttlefish eats crabs and fish.**

MOLLUSKS

Octopus

Their **suction** cups can hold food.

The tentacles can taste food.

An octopus travels slowly when searching for food. It crawls along the ocean bottom. An octopus can also go very fast. It can shoot water through its body and swim like a jet flies.

- An octopus has eight **tentacles**. They are like arms.
- The octopus can spray dark ink from its body. The ink helps it hide.
- This creature has no bones or shell.

A new tentacle grows if an old one is lost!

MOLLUSKS

Squid

FACTS

- A squid has a shell inside its body.
- The giant squid can grow 60 feet long.
- A squid can make its own light.

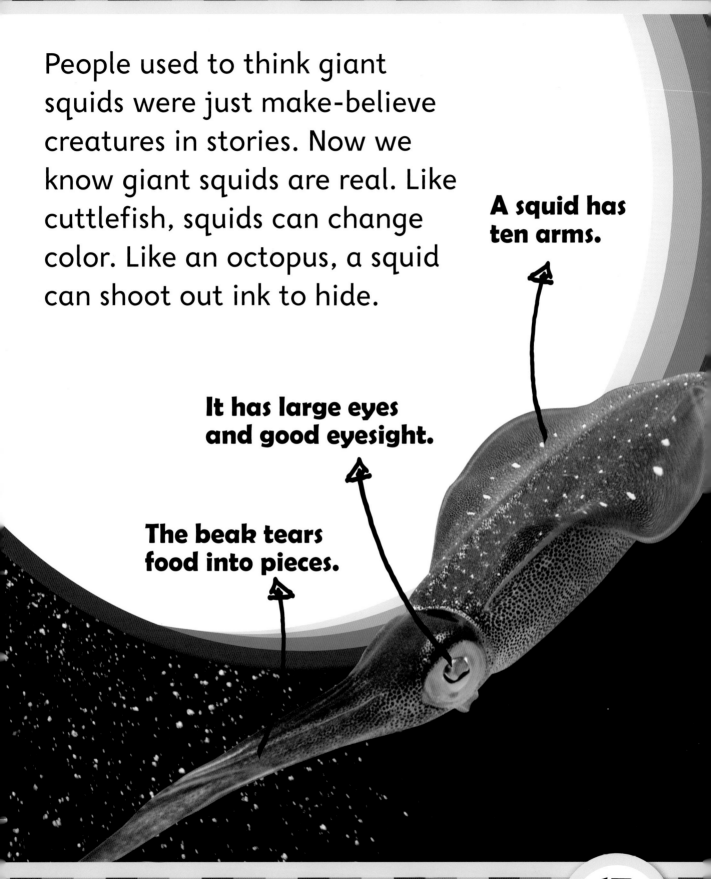

People used to think giant squids were just make-believe creatures in stories. Now we know giant squids are real. Like cuttlefish, squids can change color. Like an octopus, a squid can shoot out ink to hide.

A squid has ten arms.

It has large eyes and good eyesight.

The beak tears food into pieces.

MAMMALS

Seal

Flippers help
a seal swim.

- Seals talk by grunting, honking, or barking.
- They can swim up to 25 miles per hour.
- Seal fat is called **blubber**. It keeps the seals warm.

Whiskers help it find food.

This seal has ear flaps. Not all seals do.

Seals are great swimmers. They can stay underwater for a long time. But seals are not fish. They are mammals like you. They breathe air. They can hold their breath underwater for up to an hour.

MAMMALS

Dolphin

This body shape is good for swimming.

Dolphins are one of the smartest animals on Earth. They live in groups and help each other. A strong dolphin will push a hurt dolphin to the top of the water. Then the hurt dolphin can breathe air.

A **fin** on top helps with balance.

A dolphin breathes through a **blowhole**.

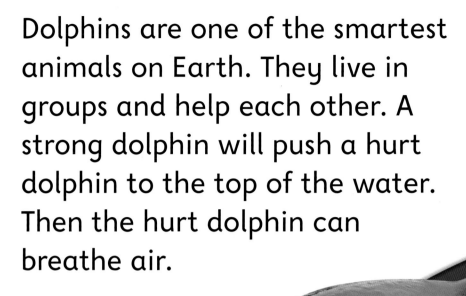

FACTS

- A dolphin looks like a fish. Yet it is a mammal.
- It talks using clicks, grunts, and squeaks.
- They make sounds that bounce off objects. The dolphin can then make sound pictures of the objects.

MAMMALS

Whale

Whales eat small fish and other marine animals.

The tail moves to help the whale swim.

FACTS

- **The blue whale is the largest animal ever. It is bigger than any dinosaur!**
- **A whale's song can be heard for miles underwater. One song can last for 30 minutes.**
- **Some whales live for 100 years.**

Whales are the biggest animals on Earth. Yet the water holds up their weight. Have you seen a whale jump high out of the water? That kind of jumping is called **breaching**.

The blowhole shoots out air and water.

CRUSTACEANS

Crab

FACTS

- A crab has ten legs. Two are claws. The rest are used for walking.

- Some crabs hide under seaweed.

- Hermit crabs cannot grow their own shells. They use shells that have been shed by other crabs.

Pincers help crabs protect themselves.

Some crabs live deep in the ocean. Yet most live at the shore. They eat small, dead animals for food. Most crabs outgrow their first shells. They **shed** those shells and grow new ones.

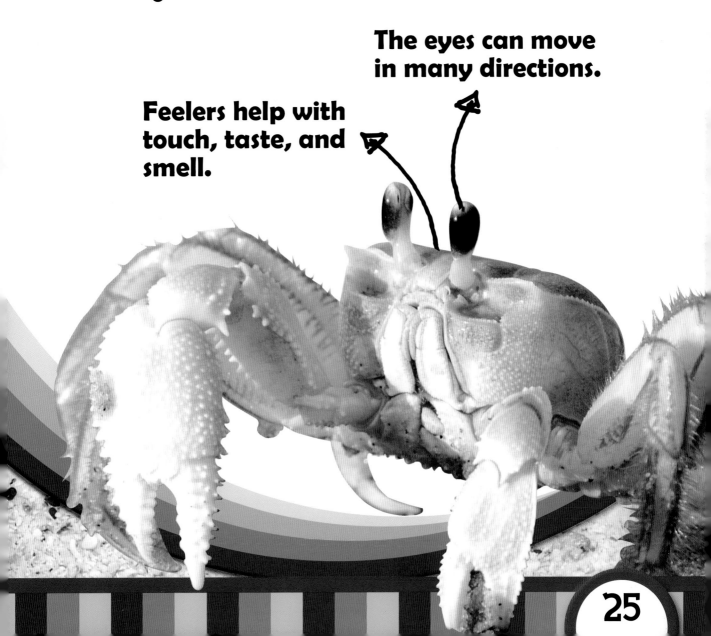

The eyes can move in many directions.

Feelers help with touch, taste, and smell.

Lobster

Feelers help it find its way around.

On lobsters, one claw is bigger than the other. The big claw is used for crushing shells to get to food. The small claw is used for cutting food into pieces. Both claws help the lobster fight.

It tastes food with its feet!

FACTS

- **Each lobster has three stomachs.**
- **A lobster carries its eggs around instead of leaving them in a nest.**
- **The tail moves to help it go backward or forward.**

CRUSTACEANS

Giant Isopod

Large eyes help an isopod see in the dark.

Giant isopods crawl along the bottom of the ocean. They eat whatever falls down that far. They eat dead whales, fish, and squids. A hungry isopod will eat and eat until it cannot move.

- A giant isopod lives in the deep part of the ocean. It is found 2,000 feet down.
- If **threatened**, it rolls into a tight ball. A hard shell then protects it.
- An isopod can live for up to eight weeks without eating.

There are two sets of **antennae**.

The hard shell is strong but can bend.

Glossary

antennae–feelers on the head of an animal

blowhole–hole that ocean mammals breathe through

blubber–fat in sea mammals

breaching–breaking through; a whale breaking through water

crustaceans–water animals with a hard shell and "arms" with joints

fin–flat, outer body part of a fish or an ocean mammal that helps with swimming and balance

fish–water animals with a backbone (or spinal column) and fins

flaps–pieces of skin on animals

flippers–flat limbs good for swimming

mammals–animals that breathe air and give birth to babies, not eggs

mollusks –water animals with a soft body typically covered by a shell

pincers–claws on some kinds of animals

schools–groups of fish that stay together

seaweed–a plant that grows in the ocean

shed–get rid of

suction–being able to stick

tentacles–animal parts much like arms

threatened–placed in danger

whiskers–long, stiff hairs or items like hair

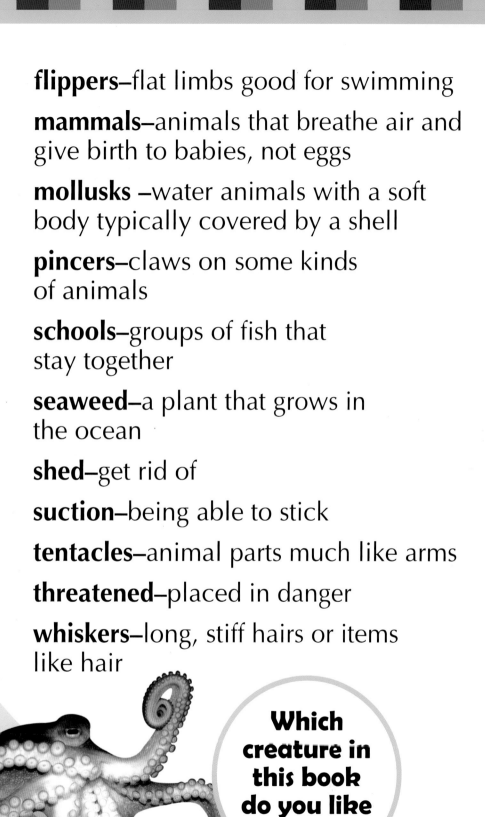

Which creature in this book do you like best?

Index